DECLUTTER YOUR INBOX

9 Proven Steps to Eliminate Email Overload

By S.J. Scott

http://www.HabitBooks.com

January 2014
Copyright © 2014 S.J. Scott
All rights reserved worldwide.

Published by Archangel Ink

ISBN 1496001079
ISBN-13: 978-1496001078

Disclaimer

Table of Contents

Why You Should Declutter Your Inbox

Are you overwhelmed by email? Don't have enough time to work on important projects? Keep missing important messages?

In our hectic work and personal lives, it's easy to get buried under the avalanche of messages sitting in your inbox. While email can enhance your business communication, it can also become overwhelming and often turn into a huge time sink.

Odds are if you're reading this book, then you've probably experienced the challenge of being overwhelmed by email while trying to remain productive.

Let email control you and it could lead to:

- Low productivity
- Stress
- Distraction
- Lack of focus on important projects

Email can even be a burden for high-powered executives. In fact, according to the Mckinsey Global Institute (http://www.mckinsey.com/insights/high_tech_teleco ms_internet/the_social_economy), executives spend an average of 28 percent of their workdays managing email. Do the math on that. That's more than two hours every day, 13 hours per week, 50 hours per month and 675 hours per year. **The grand total is 28 days per year – on email!**

So imagine spending ALL of February, day and night, doing nothing but answering emails.

Crazy, right?

It has been said that there is an inverse relationship between email and productivity. Many personal development experts feel the less time you spend on email, the more productive you can become. Leo Babauta, the owner of *Zen Habits*, simply "quit" email altogether (check out this post for more information http://zenhabits.net/killing-email-how-and-why-i-ditched-my-inbox/).

As much as you might like to declare "email bankruptcy," it's not socially acceptable (or a smart career move) to tell people you'll no longer answer their messages. You live in the real world. People rely on you to answer your email.

On top of the time spent on email, you probably deal with other distractions from the modern world: Twitter, Facebook, Tumblr, Pinterest, Instagram, LinkedIn, instant messaging and blogging. What's amazing *isn't* how much time we waste. It's how we're able to get anything done at all.

This is where the "declutter your inbox" habit comes into play.

Whereas most books (and blog posts) recommend fancy technology to help stem the tide of email, this solution doesn't solve the root problem. It's kind of like a doctor focusing on the symptoms, not the disease. In order to do your best work in a peaceful, constructive manner, you need to develop a specific routine that focuses on email efficiency.

By applying a few core strategies, busy executives can turn two hours of email time into 30 minutes. Others can turn a 50-minute email session into 15 minutes. And the rest of us can simply streamline our "inbox time" and get back lost time that can be spent doing the important things in life.

There are many people who have written about this subject of controlling email. Merlin Mann (http://www.43folders.com/), David Allen (http://www.davidco.com/), Lifehacker (http://lifehacker.com/) authors and Leo Babauta (http://zenhabits.net/about/) have all tackled the subject and given decent frameworks for reducing the amount of time wasted managing email.

The problem?

There is *so much* available information it's hard to identify the *simplest* way to process email.

Fortunately, there is good news. I have read through countless books and blog posts on this topic. I've applied a number of strategies in my life, throwing out what doesn't work. And finally, I've come up with a simple framework that anyone can use to streamline the time that's spent in your inbox.

The end result is *Declutter Your Inbox: 9 Proven Steps to Eliminate Email Overload.*

The step-by-step plan in this book will help you—no matter how many emails you receive on a daily basis. If you are someone who only spends 20 minutes managing email, the tips in this book will help you cut that time in half. On the other hand, if you are a high-powered executive who spends as much as three to four hours per day managing email, this book will help you discover a number of high-leverage habits that will increase your productivity.

Regardless of your personal need, you will find a wide variety of tips, ideas and strategies that will leave you with an empty inbox at the end of every day.

Who am I?

You might wonder who I am and why I feel uniquely qualified to talk about email productivity.

My name is S.J. Scott. I run the blog Develop Good Habits (http://www.developgoodhabits.com/). The goal of my site is to show how *continuous* habit development can lead to a better life. One of my primary goals is to provide simple strategies you can easily incorporate into your busy life. It's been my experience that the best way to make a lasting change is to develop one quality habit at a time.

I have run a number of online businesses in the last decade, with multiple blogs and over 30 Kindle books in Amazon's marketplace. Every day that my "brand" grows, I get to meet and talk to more people.

The problem?

Six months ago, I reached my breaking point when it came to email.

Although I *love* interacting with everyone, it has gotten progressively harder to keep up with the flood of email in my inbox. On some days, I get anywhere from 100 to 200 emails. At one point, I was spending over three hours each day on email, and every hour that I spent in my inbox was an hour that I wasn't creating content.

Eventually, I had two choices:

First, I could become one of those "lifestyle guys" who only replies with elaborate autoresponders and expects people to jump through a million hoops to get a moment of my precious time. For example, I could have sent the following:

"Thanks for your email. I only answer messages every Monday between 1:00 p.m. and 2:00 p.m. (Kaliningrad Time). Please arrange an appointment with my personal assistant, and then send a message during this window of time. She'll screen the message using a 16-point checklist. If your email matches all 16 points on my list, I'll get back to you."

The other option was to get *really* good at processing email, developing an efficient system that would allow me to process email quickly without losing the human element that is so important for growing a business.

My choice, of course, was the second option.

While it hasn't been easy, I've developed a reliable system that's worked for me, which I've turned into the blueprint you're about to read.

For many months, I have studied, researched, tested and filtered out what doesn't work.

All of this is presented in a simple, easy-to-digest format.

If you're looking to develop a habit to help you reduce the amount of time spent in your inbox, then keep reading to find out how you can be more productive.

6 Limiting Beliefs about Email

Getting a handle on your inbox starts *before* you check email. In order to end every day with a clear conscience, you'll need to address the underlying psychology behind how you view email. In this section we'll cover six limiting beliefs many people have about email.

They're called "limiting beliefs" simply because they *limit* your ability to do great work. Rather than spending your time focused on important projects, it's often easier to respond to that *ding* of a new message and immediately respond to it—kind of like a rat chasing down a piece of cheese.

If you want an empty inbox on a consistent basis, you first have to address these six limiting beliefs. Some of them might not apply to you, but take the time to look at each one and decide if you're making these mistakes.

Limiting Belief #1: You Must Be Constantly Available

Without a doubt, the biggest limiting belief of our modern world is the idea that we need to *"always be available."* Technology makes it possible to connect with others 24 hours per day, seven days per week, and 365 days per year. Therefore, people sometimes feel like they need to respond instantly to every email, text message and phone call.

This is just not true.

Yes, being chained to technology keeps you connected to the world, but it also prevents you from giving your full attention to a project or spending quality time with the important people in your life.

If you truly want success, then you need to focus and stop being a slave to your inbox.

That means eliminating the habit of checking email every few minutes.

Now, I understand monitoring email might be an important part of your job, so it's up to you to decide how often you'll check in. The important lesson here is you need to schedule specific times each day to go through your email messages.

Overall, my experience has been that most professional people (probably you) tend to check their email far more than necessary.

Xobni – the company that created Outlook – recently conducted a study to determine how people use email. Nearly 75 percent of the people who participated said they check their business email at home, while "relaxing" on vacation, before bed and as soon as they wake up in the morning. That's madness!

Email has invaded every aspect of our lives. For success, happiness and long-term sanity, you must take control of your inbox.

My suggestion?

Schedule time to process your email each day. If you receive fewer than 20 messages per day, you shouldn't need to check your email more than once. If you receive 20 to 50 messages daily, check your email no more than three times per day. If you receive a high volume of messages, or your success hinges on timely email responses, then four to five times per day will work.

I generally recommend checking your email no more than twice per day—once in the late morning and once at the end of the day.

Unless you work in customer service, there's really no need to worry about sending immediate responses to the emails you receive. The earth will not tilt off its axis and come to a fiery end if someone has to wait two hours for a reply to their question.

Responding to email in the late morning lets you spend that first part of each day working on your top projects. Doing it at the end of the day allows you to put out all the fires that happened during the workday and wrap things up. Then you can go home with a clear conscience and not feel guilty about any lingering, unanswered message.

Is there a "right" time for these two email sessions?

Not really.

When you process email depends on your specific schedule and the nature of your job. I recommend the late morning and late afternoon time slots because they bookend your day.

The key here is to get the best results from a full day's work between the sessions. You clear messages twice a day so you can spend the rest of your time on the important parts of your job.

We'll come back to this subject later on, and I'll show you how to build habits that counter those "urges" to constantly check your email.

Limiting Belief #2: Feeling "Guilty"

When someone reaches out to you, it's rude to not respond. I know my mother taught me it's always polite to respond to people when they initiate a conversation.

The flip side of that mindset is it's also rude to start a conversation if it's obvious that someone is busy or in the middle of another conversation.

When you boil it all down:

"Email interactions should happen when both parties are ready to fully engage in the conversation."

The problem with modern technology is it's easy to forget that an email is often an interruption to your day. Therefore, it's easy to think it's rude to *not* respond as quickly as possible. This is 100 percent wrong. Email is not a conversation. The other party can't tell if you are busy, swamped with work or "in the zone" when they click send. If you have this limiting belief, you will still feel guilty if you're not responding to every email within a few minutes.

To illustrate this point, let's talk about the television show *Hoarders*.

This program focuses on people who are unable to "let go" of their personal possessions. They keep things in massive piles until their lives become completely unmanageable. They experience a great deal of guilt over throwing anything out away, until they're literally surrounded by mountains of junk.

The easy answer is to tell these people to get rid of their stuff, but it's equally easy to forget about the guilt some people experience when they get rid of their possessions.

My point?

Many people – maybe even you – feel guilty about not taking action on specific messages. So you ignore the problem and let the messages build up in your inbox. It becomes harder and harder to keep track of the truly important things, which leads to more guilt and ratchets the whole problem up another notch. The end result is you're sitting on the digital version of *Hoarders*.

Like on *Hoarders*, your best bet is to systematically process everything one time and then develop the empty-inbox habit that will keep things from ever getting out of control.

As we go through the exercises in this book, you might feel guilt because of the following reasons:

• Not checking email 10 times per day like other people

- Giving brief, actionable responses to people who write page-long messages
- Only responding at specific times during the day
- Using template responses to generic questions
- Deleting pointless promotional messages
- Canceling your subscriptions to free email newsletters

Again, we'll go into the specifics of each of the above items. The important thing to remember is it's *your* life. That means you should never let someone else make you feel guilty because you've made the decision to take control of your inbox.

Limiting Belief #3: Short Emails Are Rude

It is easy to fall into the trap of thinking short emails are rude. This is especially true when someone sends you the email equivalent of *War and Peace.*

Honestly, I feel long emails are disrespectful of my time. They take a long time to read and an even longer to time to reply to. It can be particularly frustrating if I feel the sender could have answered their own question with a simple Google search.

At the risk of sounding harsh (if I haven't done that already), many people are lazy when it comes to the Send button. They won't take the time to research their own questions, but they expect you to drop what you're doing and provide detailed responses to every email.

To fully develop the empty-inbox habit, you need to eradicate the notion that giving short answers is rude. As you'll learn later on, your job is to kill the fluff and stifle the impulse to provide lengthy replies. That means if a question requires a one-sentence response, then that's <u>all</u> you need to write.

Unnecessarily verbose replies waste both your time and the recipient's time. Answer fully, but with as few words as possible. Get to the point and get out.

Limiting Belief #4: Thinking Other People Are More Important Than Your Own Priorities

Email has evolved over time. Most of what you get isn't immediately important, yet we all feel the impulse to immediately act on it. To put it succinctly, your average email is *urgent, but not important.*

The best illustration of this point can be found in the teachings of time-management expert Stephen Covey. One of his classic beliefs is you can divide all work into four basic categories:

	Urgent	Not Urgent
Important	Crying baby Kitchen fire Some calls 1	Exercise Vocation Planning 2
Not Important	3 Interruptions Distractions Other calls	4 Trivia Busy work Time wasters

(Image provided courtesy of Wikimedia.)

Most messages fall firmly into the third and fourth boxes of Covey's chart. While they might deserve a response, they need to be acted on when *you* have the time to respond, not the other way around.

Don't get me wrong; I believe it's important to be helpful and treat others with respect, but you should never label every single message as "urgent" and drop what you're doing to act on one.

Limiting Belief #5: Using an Inbox Like a To-Do List

One *big* mistake I see many people make is treating their email inboxes like an ad hoc "to-do list."

If you're like most people, you will never complete your entire to-do list. Odds are you're constantly thinking of new ideas and fun projects to start, so there's never enough time to get to everything. What this means is if you treat your email like a to-do list, you'll never truly empty your inbox.

The "inbox to-do list" mentality can have a negative impact on your productivity. Whenever you open up your inbox, you'll see those unfinished projects staring you in the face. This takes up mental capacity, creating stress and anxiety that carry over into your work.

One interesting example that supports this idea comes from studies done on the *Zeigarnick effect*. The idea here is that **every unfinished task takes up a certain amount of your focus**. Even if you're *not* consciously thinking about an incomplete task, some part of your brain is churning away in the background.

Although you don't need to take immediate action on every single email, you need to develop a system to ensure you complete the appropriate action in a timely manner. Only then will you treat your inbox as a communication device—not a productivity tool. (If you want to learn more about the *Zeigarnick effect,* check out this blog post where I discuss the concept. (http://www.developgoodhabits.com/zeigarnik-effect/)

When it comes to to-do lists, I'm a low-tech guy. I print out my list at the start of each week and write down – with an amazing tool called a "pen" – the new tasks that pop up every day.

On the other hand, you might use software or an app to manage a to-do list. It doesn't matter *what* you use. What matters is keeping tasks out of your inbox.

Now, this book doesn't cover to-do lists, so I'll simply say you can use any of the following to manage your day-to-day activities:

- Evernote
- Notebooks
- iPad/iPhone/tablet apps
- Index cards
- Post-It Notes
- Microsoft Excel spreadsheets

Later on, we'll talk about the "4 D's of email processing." For now, the important takeaway is to remember that your inbox isn't the place for actions. An email should be unopened or acted upon. Period.

Limiting Belief #6: "Email Bankruptcy" is the Answer

When someone gets deep into debt, often the only legal recourse is to declare bankruptcy. The same can be said for the digital world. It's very common for people to let their email get so out of hand that the simplest action is to "select all" and hit the delete button. This is called email bankruptcy.

While email bankruptcy *is* an option, it's usually not the best one. I think of it as similar to killing the patient to cure the disease. Deleting every email isn't a solution; it's sweeping the problem under the rug.

I'll admit there is some validity to the idea that if something is important, people will email you a second time. However, it's dangerous to assume you won't miss out on an email that might be important.

A far better solution is to develop habits that reshape your attitude toward email. Once you learn the routines that effectively control email, you'll *do more in less time* and email will never get to that point where you feel tempted to declare bankruptcy.

So what are these habits?

In the next section, we'll go over the seven habits you can use to declutter your inbox and keep it that way.

7 Habits to Declutter Your Inbox

Anyone can delete email. The hard part is building habits to help you quickly sort, respond and take action on messages, *without* wasting your time. This is why it's important to build an actionable system that allows you to manage an inbox in a streamlined fashion.

That said, creating an "email system" won't fix the underlying problem of why you struggle to maintain an empty inbox. It's kind of like slapping a Band-Aid on a severe wound. It's a temporary fix, which makes it easy to revert back to the old habits that caused your email problem.

Think of it this way. Let's say you clean your house just one time. The house might look nice for a little while, but without a fundamental, internal change, you'll quickly go back to your messy habits. A better long-term solution is to build good email "housekeeping" habits that will help you clean your inbox today and keep it clutter-free for years to come.

In this section, we'll talk about seven of these habits. None of them are tough to develop, but they do take time to integrate into a daily routine. While you can try to do all of them at once, I recommend focusing on building one – or maybe two – at a time.

Many experts say it takes a minimum of 21 to 30 days to start a new habit, so I recommend focusing on each of the following in a systematic manner. To learn more about this concept, check out the 30-day habit challenge series on my blog (http://www.developgoodhabits.com/30-day-habit-challenge/).

Now, let's go over each of these seven habits.

Habit #1: Schedule Email Processing Time(s)

Habits require specificity. You can't say, *"I will check my email in the morning"* and expect to follow through every single day. Habits are built by consistently doing the same thing at the same time. The best way to empty an inbox every day is to schedule time dedicated to this task.

How often and *when* you do this is up to you, but I urge you to be extremely specific to make it work.

The hardest part of mastering this habit is pulling the plug on the one thing that often feeds an inbox addiction: email notifications.

You know what I'm talking about. These are those dinging sounds you hear and pop-ups you see whenever a new message lands in your inbox. Pavlov would be proud because these stimuli (sounds) generally elicit a response (checking your email).

The only way to truly break this vicious cycle is to remove free will from the equation by turning off *all* email notifications. Do this one step and you'll get back a huge amount of time that can be spent on important projects.

To illustrate this point, here are a few good reasons to schedule time to process your inbox:

1. Batching similar tasks together makes them easier to process.
2. Scheduling processing time makes it easier to organize your day.
3. People will often answer their own questions because they won't get an immediate response, saving you time and effort.
4. If you have only a short amount of time to process your email, you'll have a ticking clock that reminds you to be efficient.
5. You'll develop an intuitive understanding of how to respond to specific types of messages.

Managing email is like doing any other task. During the first few minutes, you'll feel sluggish and out of sync, but eventually you'll get into a rhythm where you respond to each message in a rapid-fire manner. By processing your email only a few times a day, you'll do it efficiently and avoid getting distracted by other tasks.

Before responding to *any* message, think for a few seconds about how much back and forth is needed. Ask yourself the following:

- Are there going to be questions?
- Is the topic easy to follow?
- Will the recipient need more clarification?
- Is it even possible to follow the five-sentence rule?

Will this conversation lead to a ping pong, back-and-forth interaction?

This step is important because often email *isn't* the best tool for certain conversations. If you can't describe an outcome in a few sentences or provide a pre-written response, then a simpler solution is to schedule a five-minute conversation over the phone or via Skype.

It's easy to love the simplicity of email, but we often rely on it to do too much. By stopping and collecting your thoughts before each email, you'll figure out if replying is the best use of your time. If a response requires a lengthy conversation, then you can schedule a quick conversation to go over the important points.

The question is: How do you know if an email only requires a quick response?

Simply look for an email that is:

- A clear question needing only a simple answer
- A generic response that can be replied to using a template

- A brief status update to a large audience
- A request for a needed file or Web link
- A confirmation of a meeting or appointment
- A problem that can be resolved by a one-time email exchange

If a message *doesn't* fit one of these parameters, then don't waste time writing a lengthy response. Instead, use one of the collaboration tools I'll discuss in a later section.

Habit #4: "Single Handle" Each Message

In an earlier section, we discussed the Zeigarnick effect and how incomplete tasks can take up a lot of your mental capacity. A simple solution to this is to create the "single handling" habit.

This concept is a derivative of what David Allen discusses in his *Getting Things Done* (GTD) book. What Allen advocates is using the "two-minute rule" for handling tasks. If something takes less than two minutes to complete, then do it immediately. Otherwise, it's better to schedule this task as a future action item.

While I think time constraints are important, I personally feel two minutes isn't enough time for many emails. Instead, I recommend establishing the "five-minute rule" for processing each message. Honestly, it's better to take care of most emails the moment you open them rather than wasting time with a follow-up action.

Whether you go with a two-minute, five-minute or even a ten-minute rule for email, the important point is to create a "mental clock" while processing your inbox so you don't get lost down the rabbit hole of spending 30 minutes on a single message.

Habit #5: Eliminate Pointless Email

Most productivity experts recommend setting aside an hour every month to unsubscribe from unimportant newsletters. *The problem?* This is such an annoying task that it's easy to put it off and simply "mass delete" junk emails on a daily basis. Unfortunately, the more you wait to delete pointless emails, the more herculean this task becomes.

A simpler solution is to regularly – at least every few days – open each message and hit the unsubscribe link or the SPAM button (for those email lists that won't let you unsubscribe). Do this on a regular basis to quickly and permanently get rid of these messages that don't add value to your life.

Personally, I treat each email as an opportunity to eliminate something new. Unless I find the information to be useful or engaging, then I take five seconds to filter that content out of my life.

Habit #6: Learn How to Touch Type

How would you rate your typing skills? Are you a quick typist? Do you use two fingers or three? Four? Six? Both hands? How many errors do you make in a typical sentence?

you're still hunting and pecking with two
on a keyboard, then you're severely limiting
ility to quickly process email.

A simple solution is to develop the *touch-typing habit*.

Develop this one habit and you'll almost *halve* your inbox time. For instance, a touch typist can produce, on average, 40 to 60 words per minute. On the other hand, a hunt-and-peck typist produces 25 words per minute. Extrapolate this to an hour and its 2,400 words vs. 1,500 words, which is almost a 40 percent increase in speed. You better believe this will improve your email efficiency.

Now, I'm sure that taking a typing class wasn't on your mind when you picked up this book. However, you don't have to go to school or take an expensive class to learn how to touch type. There are a number of programs that can teach you the touch-typing habit. One of my favorites is the one I used when I was a teenager: Mavis Beacon Teaches Typing. (http://www.developgoodhabits.com/mavis)[1]

Habit #7: Value Your Time

It's important to know what your time is worth. While my income varies from month to month, I always have a general "guesstimation" of what I make per month, per day and even per hour. I recommend you do the same with your life.

---

[1] That's *not* an affiliate link. I just think it's a good program that can help anyone learn how to touch type.

Here's a simple process for finding out how much you're worth:

1. Start with how much you're paid each month (before taxes).

2. Divide this by the amount of hours you *actually* work (not including breaks and days off).

3. Write down this hourly wage and put it in a prominent location.

4. Do this once per month (if your earnings fluctuate like mine).

With a little bit of math, you can pinpoint the exact dollar amount that each email "costs" you. Apply this rule to your inbox. When responding to a lengthy message, ask yourself: "Is this email *really* worth $___ of my time?"

I'm not suggesting that you take this mercenary approach with every email that crosses your path. Instead, use it as a reminder when you process those "80/20 emails"—the messages that take up the bulk of your time but offer very little value in return. When you notice that certain *types* of messages occupy most of your time, then take immediate action and process them in a more efficient manner.

Keep your hourly wage in the front of your mind while working through your inbox. This will create a sense of urgency and act as a constant reminder that your job isn't to produce stellar email content. It's to quickly help people and provide solutions. Email isn't the end or a means to the end; it's a tool to help facilitate and plan your real work.

Your Next Step:

If you can successfully develop *all* seven of these habits, you'll find it's not hard to process your inbox in an efficient manner.

That said, you shouldn't "wait" to develop all these habits before taking aggressive action on clearing the clutter out of your inbox. In a way, the above habits are higher-level strategies that can bring about a long-term change in your life.

The good news?

You can implement a specific strategy today and see an immediate improvement in how you handle email.

In the bulk of this book, I'll reveal a nine-step strategy you can use to empty your inbox today and keep it clutter-free moving forward.

Let's start with the first step of the process.

Step #1: Turn off Email Notifications

What's the *best* thing about your cell phone? It gives you the ability to communicate and be connected anywhere in the world.

What's the *worst* thing about your cell phone?

It gives you the ability to communicate and be connected anywhere in the world.

No, the above isn't a typo. The biggest benefit and drawback of the cell phone is exactly the same. When used properly, it can help you reach out and stay connected. On the other hand, it can be a constant source of workflow interruption or even ruin private moments with the people in your life.

In my opinion, one of the worst disruptors of your time is those small email notifications. It seems like whenever you're in the middle of something, you get a ding from an email, which makes you feel "incomplete" unless you immediately check this message. (Think back to our discussion on the Zeigarnick effect and how unfinished tasks can weigh on your subconscious.)

My suggestion?

Turn off the email notifications on your **phone. I recommend you also <u>completely</u> disable every inbox from your cell phone.**

As I write this section, I can imagine the horrified – even angry – response to this suggestion. You might even think I'm a nutso for suggesting such a crazy idea, but hear me out on this.

Other than writing an occasional short response, most people don't take time to reply to messages on their phones. Usually they browse their inboxes out of sheer boredom. They're not in a place where they can respond, but they feel compelled to check anyway.

The end result?

Looking at email at your phone often causes stress and anxiety because you feel like some messages require an immediate response, but you're not in a place to give one. Now imagine that you look at your phone multiple times per day (like most people do). Odds are you'll never feel completely focused on a project because in the back of your mind, you're thinking about those emails that require a response.

The main reason I recommend disabling the email feature on your phone is it forces you to open messages *only* when you're in front of the computer, ready to provide an immediate response.

Disabling email is pretty easy to figure out. Most cell phones come with a Settings feature that only takes a minute to use.

On the iPhone, for example, you can disable email by going to:

Settings --> Mail, Contacts, Calendars --> Open the specific inbox --> Select the "Delete Account" button.

Rinse and repeat for each inbox.

If you use a different phone, then you can find quick instructions by going to Google and entering: *how to disable email on* _____ (insert the model of your phone).

I'll agree that this first step is pretty extreme, but try it for a few days. You'll discover that you won't miss checking email every hour. Plus, you'll be less stressed because there won't be any lingering "unanswered" messages weighing on your subconscious mind.

Step #2: Disable *Other* Notifications

I'm sure I've already freaked out a couple of readers with the last suggestion. Now I'm going to ratchet it up a notch.

Let's face it; email isn't the only tool that makes "pinging/dinging" sounds on your computer and cell phone. Odds are you experience regular interruptions from social media, apps, software and everything else under the sun.

Honestly, the advice in this book won't work unless you take an aggressive approach to every other type of notification. The truth is you can't be productive if you're constantly distracted by pinging sounds and pop-ups every few minutes.

Let's look at the biggest culprits:

- Facebook
- Instagram
- Twitter
- YouTube
- LinkedIn

- Pinterest
- Apps (AKA "Push Notifications")
- Tumblr
- Software updates
- Other social media

All of these come with email notifications designed to make you stop what you're doing and check out their sites. I don't have anything against the above companies. My problem is they understand *how* people get distracted, so they specifically design their platform to keep you coming back for more…kind of like a drug dealer.

My suggestion?

Go to each of the sites/tools you use and disable ALL notifications—especially the emails that are sent for every message and status update. Seriously, do you really need to get an email whenever someone posts a picture of *Grumpy Cat*?

You don't have to ditch any of your favorite social sites. If you enjoy spending your free time on Twitter, Facebook or Pinterest, then don't be afraid to do so. However, you should be doing it during free time—not when you're trying to be productive. Instant messages and status updates should be part of your relaxation time, not your work time.

Set aside a few hours in the next week and go through each tool that sends notifications; then disable each one. This might take some time to do, but once this task is complete, you'll notice a lot less clutter in your inbox.

Step #3: Streamline All Your Inboxes

If you *only* have one inbox, then feel free to skip this chapter. However, if you're juggling multiple email accounts, then streamline them and send all of your email to one central location.

A few months back, I had four email accounts (personal, business #1, business #2 and business #3), plus a slew of "junk" accounts that I use for random autoresponders and email lists. That's a *lot* of email to sort on a daily basis.

One of the biggest "wins" I've achieved in my quest for permanently decluttering my inbox was creating a central location for *all* email.

Here are a few action items to help you do the same:

Action 1: Eliminate as many inboxes as possible.

First, it's important to focus on one, maybe two, inboxes every day. If possible, streamline everything down to one account. The fewer inboxes, the better.

Earlier, I mentioned that I had four email accounts. Now I maintain two—one for my personal life and one for my business. Unless you're running two separate businesses that don't fit one another, there's nothing wrong with sending every message to a single inbox.

Action 2: Use email filters.

There are some types of messages (like email newsletters) that you might want to keep, but aren't important enough to review on a daily basis. What you can do with these is filter them into specific folders in your inbox.

The benefit of this strategy is you look at these messages *only* when you have free time. They're not cluttering your inbox and they're not distracting you from the important messages.

Filtering email requires a specific technical strategy, so we'll get back to this topic at the end of this book.

Action 3: Proactively ignore certain accounts.

Ignore the things that truly don't matter.

You don't always need to read every email blast. Or every sales message. Or Amazon's "you may like" emails. Or birthday notifications from Facebook. If you haven't disabled these notifications (step #2), then it's okay to purposefully ignore the inboxes of certain accounts.

As an example, I haven't looked at a single Twitter direct message in two years. Perhaps I've missed an important message, but I don't think this is a good enough reason to sort through 99 percent of the SPAM messages that land in this particular inbox.

If possible, you can even update your social accounts with autoresponders giving information on how people can effectively and reliably contact you.

Action 4: Create a system for processing each inbox.

After streamlining your inboxes into a central location, follow this strategy on a daily basis:

1. Stick to your once- or twice-a-day check.
2. Go through each inbox until it has been processed completely (remember, this is how you develop a single-handling habit).
3. Use a bottom-top approach. Start with the oldest message. Take the appropriate action using the "4 D's" we'll discuss in the next section and move on to the next message. No skipping or cherry picking allowed. Go through each in a systematic fashion.
4. Repeat this process for each inbox.

What this step teaches you is a sense of discipline when it comes to handling email. You might think all of this is silly because replying to email *should be* an instinctive action, but following this process will help you make quick decisions and avoid the trap of cluttering your inbox.

The key point of this step is to learn how to make quick decisions about each message. Fortunately, I have a simple four-part strategy to simplify the entire process. Let's talk about that in the next section.

Step #4: Practice the 4 D's of Email Management

Pay close attention to this step for one of the most important lessons on effective email management. Whenever you're processing an inbox, you want to use the "4 D's":

1. Delete
2. Delegate
3. Do it
4. Defer it

There is no "let me think about it" or "deal with it tomorrow" or "find out more info." You either take the appropriate action or you schedule a time to follow up.

The 4 D's process is a simple, but elegant solution to great inbox management, so let's talk about each of the decisions you could make on an email.

Choice 1: Delete It

The delete button is your friend, not your enemy. If a message doesn't require an action or contains irrelevant information, then it's okay to delete it from your life.

What if you *might* need an email in the future? A simple solution is to create a habit where you maintain folders for certain types of information. For instance, you could create folders for the following:

- Important contact information or telephone numbers
- Tracking numbers and sales receipts
- Old conversations that might be important
- Documents and resources
- Miscellaneous and assorted items

Get in the habit of immediately categorizing email and putting messages in the appropriate folders. Once you do this a few times, you'll realize there isn't any reason to keep email in your inbox. If a message doesn't require action, you either delete it or save it for future reference.

One final point…

While it's tempting to hit the delete button on pointless messages, it's better to take five seconds to open them up and hit the unsubscribe link. I know we already talked about this topic, so I won't beat you over the head with it. The important thing to remember is to use the "4 D's" as an opportunity to regularly rid yourself of email that doesn't add value to your life.

Choice 2: Delegate It

You might think only high-level executives have the ability to delegate certain tasks. The truth is, the virtual world makes it easy for almost anyone to delegate time-consuming tasks to someone else. Even if you don't have an immediate subordinate or virtual assistant, you might have a co-worker who is better suited to handle a specific task or question.

There are a number of reasons why you should delegate a task:

1. You can focus on your expertise, not attempt to learn someone else's.
2. You increase the time spent on important tasks.
3. You can educate, guide and challenge subordinates with the delegated tasks.
4. You have one less thing to worry about on a daily basis.

As an example, I often get questions that have nothing to do with my business. Like "how can I build a website using HTML 5?" Stuff like that. I'm not a Web designer, yet I often get specific questions about the website-building process. So I've learned how to "delegate" these types of questions by directing the sender to useful websites and services that can help them out.

So how can you start to use the power of delegation in your life?

Here are three quick suggestions:

Suggestion #1: Select the task and match it to the right person. I am sure you don't enjoy being given a task that is either beneath or above you. Tasks should challenge people, not overwhelm them.

Whether you use outsourcing or delegate to a co-worker, take time to understand what skills are needed to help the person. Otherwise you're wasting the time of everyone involved.

Suggestion #2: Supervise, advise and coach.
Delegating a task removes it from your inbox, but it doesn't absolve you of all responsibility. If you're in a management position, you need to maintain a degree of control and ensure that the sender is *actually* being helped by having their email delegated to someone else.

No matter where you send the person, it's important to follow up and make sure the appropriate action has been taken.

Suggestion #3: Use software to delegate tasks. If you're someone who does a lot of delegating, then it makes sense to invest in software that helps track tasks *without* filling your inbox with non-actionable email. The following tools can clear tasks from your plate and give you reminders to follow up at a later date.

Boomerang (http://www.boomeranggmail.com/): Out of all three of these programs, my favorite is *Boomerang*, which is a free Gmail add-on for the Firefox and Chrome browsers.

Boomerang allows you to do quite a few neat tricks with email, but I think its strongest function is within the "delegate" option.

When you delegate a task, you can set up a reminder that gets the message out of your inbox and only pops up when the appropriate person *hasn't* gotten back from you. Or you can choose the option where the message is automatically deleted after a set amount of time has passed.

Another great feature of *Boomerang* is you can compose messages now and set a date (or time) to send them out in the future. With this option, you can create a series of reminders for a subordinate without having to do any additional work.

Followup.cc (http://www.followup.cc/): If you don't have Gmail, then *followup.cc* might be the tool for you. It's similar to Boomerang because it allows you to set email reminders for a future date. You can also send an email to this service and have it ping you back with a reminder at a specific date or time.

Followupthen.com (http://www.followupthen.com/): *Followupthen* is a service with a function similar to the one offered by *followup.cc*.

It doesn't matter *how* you delegate tasks. What's important is to always make sure that emails are being redirected to the person with the right skills for the job.

Choice 3: Defer It

Deferring tasks is a key step to quickly processing email. While you can delete and delegate to your heart's content, there will always be certain tasks that require a huge block of your time (usually anything over five minutes.) When you get a message like this, the appropriate response is to immediately reply with the date and time of when you'll respond *or* a request to have a quick conversation over the phone.

Let's start with the first option.

Deferring an email requires a four-step process that removes the action from your inbox and puts it into an action file.

1. Read email and make list of the steps needed to complete it.
2. Add these items to your to-do list.
3. Reply to the person and give an approximate time when they'll get a response.
4. File the email in a "pending actions" folder for future reference.

The second step in this process is the most important one. Hopefully you've established some sort of task management system and to-do list. It's far beyond the scope of this book to spend pages and pages talking about how to manage your time. Instead, I recommend reading my book *23 Anti-Procrastination Habits* and using a tool like Evernote (http://www.evernote.com) to manage all your lists and reminders.

I recommend using Evernote to manage the bulk of your tasks. With this tool, you can set reminders and create lists based on specific projects. What I really like about Evernote is that it seamlessly works on multiple platforms, so you can set a reminder on your desktop and then have access to it from your cell phone or tablet.

Now, while Evernote is my preference for managing to-do lists and multiple projects, there are a number of other options you can use. Here are a few different tools to make your life easier:

- Microsoft Excel (http://office.microsoft.com/en-us/excel/)
- Remember the Milk (http://www.rememberthemilk.com/)
- Google Docs (https://docs.google.com)
- Producteev (https://www.producteev.com/)
- Cozi (http://www.cozi.com/)
- Microsoft OneNote (http://office.microsoft.com/en-us/onenote/)
- Asana (https://asana.com/)
- Trello (https://trello.com/)
- Azendoo (https://www.azendoo.com/)
- Basecamp (https://basecamp.com/)

You'll find that the options above vary in their scope, functionality *and* price, so you should find the tool that best fits the nature of your job.

Choice 4: Do It

I have to admit—this is my favorite option. Generally speaking, it's best to take immediate action and not add yet another task to your to-do list. This goes back to our conversation of "single-handling" certain tasks. When you can read an email, give an immediate response and then delete the message, you'll reduce the amount of "stuff" that has to be done.

We've already talked extensively about the "do it" option when it comes to an email message, so I'll recommend this simple rule:

"If an email requires a five-minute (or less) response, then take the appropriate action, reply to the sender and delete the email."

Fortunately, you'll find that most emails fall into this last category. Your average message only requires a minute or two of thinking, two minutes of writing (using the five-sentence rule) and hitting the send button.

Even if a message takes longer, you can use "template responses" to shorten the overall process. We'll get to this in a later section.

Developing the "4 D's Habit"

While it takes time to develop, the "4 D's habit" can help you make quick, efficient decisions. Do this enough and you'll learn how to quickly process an inbox.

Like other projects, it's best to focus on this activity and ignore all other distractions. That way you can do more with the same amount of time.

5: Create a Central Location for Commonly Used Files

Depending on the nature of your work, you might get constant requests for files or certain pieces of information. Responding can be a time-consuming task if you constantly have to scan through multiple folders to send a document. The solution? Create a folder on your desktop and use it to store the files people ask for via email (I call mine "Email Correspondence." Clever, right?).

Every time you send a file, think about how often you do it. If it's more than a few times a month, then put the file in a central location for future retrieval. That way, you don't have to waste 10 seconds whenever someone asks for a document.

Plus, it helps to have a "template response" for each file. Write down the information about the document (one time) and keep this on a Notepad document that's open while responding to email. That way you can cut and paste a response, add the file, tailor your message to the other person and immediately send it out. Nice and efficient.

Next, keep adding to and updating this folder. If someone requests something that's not in this folder, then take a few seconds to add it while you're responding to the sender. This will reduce your response time even more.

Finally, uploading a file can be a lengthy process. If you have the funds, you can further streamline this process by opening an Amazon AWS Account (http://aws.amazon.com/). The idea here is to upload all your commonly used files to this account and then create a template response for each one. This saves heaps of time because you're not waiting for a document to attach to an email; instead, you're giving a direct download link , hitting send and moving on to the next message.

I keep talking about the concept of the "template response," so let's talk about what that is and how you can use it to maximize email efficiency.

Step #6a: Write Template Responses for Common Emails

Ever find yourself writing the same email over and over? If so, a simple solution is to use template responses for your most commonly received messages.

Think about it this way:

If you can do a task (like answering an email) just 15 seconds faster 100 times in a week, that's a time savings of 25 minutes. Extrapolate this over the year and it grows to a total of 22 hours. Do this for the next 30 years for a total of 27 days of work. This is all from shaving a mere 15 seconds off of your daily repetitive tasks.

My point here?

Many people think giving template responses is a cold and impersonal way to connect. I have to admit, sometimes they *can* be. But I think it really depends on *what* you include in the email. You can easily create an email that's warm, personable and engaging with a line or two that's specific to the recipient. You're still conveying the same information, but you're just doing it in an efficient manner.

How do you create a template response?

First, review what you send on a regular basis, looking for common replies such as declining invitations, sending meeting requests, setting up phone conferences, attaching information and answering specific questions. Basically any email that seems "similar" deserves a template response.

Next, craft an in-depth message that answers every possible question. You can use a response that you've sent in the past as the framework, and then add as much relevant information as possible.

Finally, create broad categories for your responses. This is important because you might want to add some diversity to your messages depending on what's being asked and who the recipient is. That way you can tailor the reply to the individual and not sound so mechanical.

To get an idea of this concept, here are a few template responses that I commonly send:

Example 1: File request. We've already talked about this, but most office jobs require you to share files. I'd say in a given day, I'm asked for at least a *dozen* different files that weren't successfully sent through an autoresponder, so I keep them all in a central location and reply with any pertinent information about the document.

Example 2: Question or advice. I keep a set of common questions in a file. If I get a question I haven't heard yet (and I think it might come up again), I'll add it to this file. Basically this is my own personal FAQ. All I have to do is figure out what's *really* being asked and send the appropriate response.

Example 3: "Can't help." Some questions are simply beyond my level of expertise, so it makes sense to delegate the response to a resource that can actually help the recipient.

For instance, I often get legal questions or in-depth questions about setting up an LLC. Since I'm *not* a lawyer, I use a few templates that basically say, "I don't know" but then direct the sender to a few websites that can help.

Example 4: "No" responses. I get requests all the time for projects that simply don't fit in with what I'm doing. Things like a request to review a book, promote an affiliate offer or partner with someone in a joint venture. While some of these requests might be great, I simply don't have the time to handle them all and still complete my own projects.

To keep from getting bogged down with these requests, I've developed a nice, but firm, response. I always add personalization to the negative reply because there is a living, breathing person on the other end of the email. Then I finish the message with "I hope you understand" (credit to Steve Pavlina [http://www.stevepavlina.com] for this excellent idea).

Example 5: Phone conversation requests. If someone wants to Skype or talk on the phone, I'm usually flexible. However, there are days/times when I have to be inflexible (like mornings for writing and weekends for my personal time).

Whenever I get a request to talk on the phone, I reply with the days and times that I can talk. Otherwise, I found that people tend to pick conversation times that conflict with the time I need to work on important projects.

Example 6: Thank-you messages. This one is actually the hardest to turn into a template response because if someone sends a flattering email, I should take the time to personally listen and respond. Usually, I keep a handful of set replies, but I'll spend extra time reading the message and seeing if there's a way I can help the sender.

Those are just six examples of responses that I use. Odds are whatever you write will be vastly different from mine. The important thing is to identify common emails, write a few responses and add to this collection as new messages come in.

At this point, you might think that sending template responses can be tedious. Fortunately, there are a few shortcuts you can use to speed up the process. We'll talk about that in the next section.

Step #6b: Use Software to Post Template Responses

Most people keep their template responses in a single file, then cut and paste the information into each message. I think this is an inefficient process because every major email client has the functionality to let you give quick responses.

In this section, I'll break down the basic directions on how to set up templates in five of the major email clients: Gmail, Outlook, Yahoo!, Apple and Thunderbird.

Obviously, technology is always changing, so if these instructions don't match what's on the screen, then do a Google search to get updated information.

I: Template Responses in Gmail

Gmail uses what is known as "Canned Responses." Here is a step-by-step breakdown of how to set one up:

1. Click on the *Gear* icon.
2. Go to *Settings*.

3. Click on the *Labs* tab.
4. Type *Canned Responses* into the *Search for Lab* block.
5. Click the *Enable* button.
6. Save your changes.

At this point, Gmail is set up for canned responses, but you still need to create individual responses for each type of message.

How to *Write* a Canned Response

1. Click the *Compose* button.
2. Write your canned response.
3. Click the little arrow in bottom right corner of the screen when you've completed the Canned Response.
4. Go to *Canned Responses* --> *New Canned Responses*.
5. Name the template.

How to *Post* a Canned Response

It's easy to use a Canned Responses once you create it. Simply reply to the email and do the following:

Compose --> Canned Responses --> Choose the appropriate response.

I'll admit this can be a confusing process, so it's better to see how each of these steps looks. Here is a great WikiHow article on how to set up a Canned Response (http://www.wikihow.com/Use-Canned-Responses-in-Gmail).

...nplate Responses in Outlook

...eating a list of instructions for Outlook can be ...cause there are multiple versions in the marketplace. The following is a quick overview of how to get started:

1. Open a new message.
2. Create your template.
3. Click the *File* tab or the *Office* button.
4. Click *Save As.*
5. From the *Save As* dropdown menu, choose *Outlook Template* (*.oft).
6. Click *Save* and Outlook will save this file to the default folder.

If you get stuck, here is a brief overview of the email message template process in Outlook (http://bit.ly/18ojRAi). Also, if you use a different version of Outlook, type "*message template Outlook* [year]" in the Google search box to get the right set of instructions.

III: Template Responses in Yahoo!

At the time of this writing, Yahoo! doesn't support native templates, but there is a decent workaround for this problem. Simply keep your responses as drafts and cut and paste them into your replies.

Here's how to do this:

1. Make a folder called "Templates."
2. Send a message with the desired template text to yourself.

3. Transfer the message from the *Sent* folder to the *Templates* folder.

4. When responding to a message, open the template message in a new tab.

5. Highlight the body of the message.

6. Press Ctrl+C (Windows, Linux) or Command-C (Mac).

7. Place the cursor on the message body and hit Ctrl+V (Windows, Linux) or Command-V (Mac).

This might not save a whole lot of time like with the other email programs, but it's a decent workaround until Yahoo! decides to add the template response feature to their program.

IV: Template Responses in Apple Mail

Mac OSX and Mail.app don't have a dedicated method for supporting templates. As with Yahoo! Mail, there is a decent workaround where you can add a common response to an Apple email.

1. Make a folder called "Templates."

2. Create the template formatted the way you desire.

3. Select *File* -->Save *as Draft* from the menu.

4. Transfer the message from the *Save as Draft* folder into the *Templates* folder.

5. Use the template as a basis for future messages.

6. I'll admit this isn't a very elegant solution to using a template response in Apple, so you should also check out this page that offers a few alternative strategies (http://abt.cm/1bv6yQm).

V: Template Responses in Mozilla Thunderbird

Finally we come to the easiest system for using templates—*Mozilla Thunderbird*.

1. Design your email template.
2. Select *File --> Save As -->Template*.
3. Use the specific template when responding to a message.

Nice and easy, right?

4 Software Solutions for Template Responses

As you can see, some of these email programs can be clunky. Often, they're not straightforward or easy to understand. You might need to take some time to tinker with your email client to develop the habit of efficiently using template responses.

That said, I know some readers are "power emailers" who typically send hundreds of messages per day. For these people, using the template responses of an email client can actually *waste* time instead of saving it.

If you deal with a large amount of email every day, then it makes sense to invest in a software solution that specializes in templates and rapid email duplication.

Here are a few options:

ToutApp (http://www1.toutapp.com/original): Uses templates, scheduling and tracking to streamline your email processing time.

Rule 2: Use bold text and numbered lists.

If an email requires a lengthy response, then it's best to use bold text and/or numbered lists. This allows the recipient to scan the message and know what specific actions need to be taken. Write an email in this format and you'll avoid the back-and-forth messages that often happen when something is properly clarified.

Rule 3: Write precise subject lines.

The subject line should give the recipient a "Cliff's Notes" version of what you're trying to communicate.

"A quick question…" doesn't tell you anything, but *"3 things I need by the end of the day"* gets right to the point. Some other examples could include *"Steve Scott – Vacation days [FYI]," "Phone Conversation [Appointment],"* or *"TPS Report [Archive this]."*

With any luck, the people you regularly talk to will adapt to your system and start making their emails easier to follow.

Another thing to add to a subject line is the actions that need to be taken. For instance, you could use these modifiers: [Action items], [FYI], [Need ASAP], [Appointment] or [No reply needed]. These modifiers provide quick information on why the email is being sent and what should be done with it. Honestly, I believe that if everyone in the world used modifiers, we'd spend a lot less time on email.

Rule 4: Minimize useless replies.

If you receive an action item or don't need anything else from the sender, it's fine to reply with "got it" or something along those lines. Besides that, don't feel compelled to keep replying back and forth with pointless email. Like "thanks," "cool" or "sounds good." As long as the other person knows everything is copacetic, then it makes no sense to keep killing digital trees.

Rule 5: Remove extraneous information.

If you have a long email chain and need to forward it to a third party, don't include the entire message chain. This will only confuse the recipient with pointless information. Instead, clip and quote the applicable text and include a blurb about the actions that need to be taken.

Rule 6: Stop asking open-ended questions.

Don't end emails with phrases like, "Thoughts?" If you want a conversation, then use the phone. Email should be limited to actionable items—not creating a dialog of back and forth messages.

If you have a question, keep it to what's already being discussed. For example, *What are your thoughts on Project A? Should we go with widget 1, widget 2 or widget 3?* This gives the recipient a simple question with a simple answer, and it will ultimately cut down on back and forth emails. We'll talk more later about how to collaborate on projects without wasting too much time on email.

Rule 7: Describe the specific action(s).

Many people take five paragraphs to describe what they need. My advice? Skip the preamble and get to the point as soon as possible. Introduce yourself (if you don't know the person), include a sentence or two and then list what needs to be done. This gives the reader a chance – right off the bat – to decide how to respond.

Rule 8: Avoid multi-part questions.

Nobody wants to receive a laundry list of questions and tasks. If you have 15 different questions, then it's better to get on Skype or meet in person to go over them. This is *especially* true if you've never talked to a person before. I guarantee you won't make someone happy if your first introduction is a lengthy email full of requests.

When asking questions, stick to one, two or *maybe* three at the most, and make sure they're fairly easy to answer. Otherwise, it's better to have a phone conversation and talk it over.

Rule 9: Label attachments clearly.

If you follow my suggestion from step #5, then all of your important files should be in a central location, with clearly identified names. This is especially important if you're sending these documents to someone else. "Attachment 1" doesn't describe a thing, but if you use labels like "December_2013_Workflow.pdf" or "Screenshot_Ebook_Sales.jpg," then the recipient will know exactly what they're reading and can retrieve this file for future use.

Rule 10: Practice the Five-Sentence Rule.

Above all else, do your best to practice the Five-Sentence Rule. You might not be able to do it with every email, but if you practice keeping your words to a minimum, you'll start to develop the habit of communicating in clear, concise sentences.

Step #8: Create Email Filters

At this point, you've done a lot to stem the tide of email. To be honest, the previous seven steps are enough for most people—like 95 percent of the population. What you've already learned is enough to see a significant improvement in your email efficiency.

That said, there are some people who get triple-digit emails on a daily basis. I'm talking hundreds of emails that require replies, action steps and immediate delegation. If you're one of these people, then you probably need to set up a stringent filter system that sorts and classifies your messages *before* they end up in an inbox.

The way email filtering works is setting "rules" for the different messages and sending them to specific folders based on the actions you need to take. You can sort emails in a variety of ways:

- Send certain messages to predetermined folders.
- Tag emails based on the action required.

- Automatically forward certain messages to someone else.
- Delete or archive emails after you've replied.

For instance, a common filter might relate to the members of your team. It's easy to tag actionable messages from your boss Stan and forward them to a folder called *"Stan_Action Items."*

You can use filters to prioritize email, deal with the most important items first, and then respond to similar items using template responses.

Why is filtering important?

If you have to deal with hundreds of daily emails, you don't want to switch back and forth from topic to topic. With proper filtering, you can open one folder, deal with it completely, wipe it from your mind and move on to the next folder. It's more efficient to work this way because you're opening and closing loops in a systematic manner.

What's the best way to filter an email?

You have lots of options when it comes to filtering email, but there are three common rules that can be set.

1. From/To/CC addresses in the email header
2. Specific words or phrases in the email body
3. Attached files with the same name

You can set these filters for the presence or absence of any of these conditions. All of them rely on the typical Boolean logic: *Not, any, all, or.*

For instance, I write habit e-books. Let's say I wanted to filter messages from customers into a specific folder. I could set a rule where if an email has the phrase "your book" it would be automatically sent to a folder called "Habit Book Customers."

I could also send other messages to a separate folder. For instance, let's say I set up a filter that says if an email doesn't have "your" **and** "book," it would be sent to a folder called "Other Email Messages." Really, the way messages are filtered depends on your specific situation. They're kind of like template responses: when you see a pattern in email messages, you want to filter the most common messages with an easy-to-process system.

How do multiple filters work?

Things get tricky when you apply multiple filters. If you've set up two rules that contradict one another, then your email client will default to the first filter you've established.

For instance, if you set a rule to delete all messages from someone (let's call him Sam) and then you create a second rule where you filter his messages into a special folder, then Sam's email will never go to that folder because it will have been deleted first. The lesson here is to take time to set up each filter and make sure they seamlessly work with one another. To showcase filters, let's talk about the three major (free) email clients so you can play around with them and get a handle on how they work.

I: Filtering with Gmail

To get started, go here:

"Gear" Icon --> Settings --> Filters --> Create New Filter

From there, Gmail provides a list of options for your filter.

From: Filter based on specific email senders. They can be groups like Pinterest, Twitter or Facebook. Although these might already be under the "Social" tab, you can send them to another folder. You can also filter messages from certain people and send them to a dedicated folder.

To: This is separate from the POP3 forwarding you might have on your Gmail account. With this filter, you can forward certain messages to somewhere else in addition to the recipient. As an example, when you send an email to your assistant, you can also deliver it to another inbox where you archive all interactions.

Subject: This option will filter any message that contains a specific word or phrase in the subject line.

Has the words: Like the above, this filter will identify any word or phrase in a message and send the message to a predetermined folder.

Has attachment/include chats: These are checkboxes where you can filter messages based on what's attached or remove personal chats you've had with the recipient.

Once you've figured out *what* to filter, you'll move on to the next step. Simply click the *Continue* button and then decide what you want to do with the email. The options include *Archive, Star, Mark as Read,*

Applying Any Labels, Forward, Delete, Spam, Never Send to Spam, Mark as Important and *Categorize.* Select one of these options and press the *Create Filter* button.

Don't worry if all this sounds confusing. If you get stuck with any step, then I recommend watching this video that walks you through the entire process (http://www.youtube.com/watch?v=qRgewmaSces).

I'm not going to go into all the if/then operations of the other two email providers since they work in a similar fashion to Gmail. However, I'll describe how you can easily find the filters on each of these platforms.

II: Filtering with Hotmail

Options --> More Options --> Customize your Mail --> Automatically Sort E-Mail into Folders --> New Filter

III: Filtering with Yahoo!

Options --> More Options (top right corner) *--> Filters --> Add Filter* (top bar)

How can filters help you maintain an empty inbox?

Before we move on to the next step, let's sum up this chapter with two reasons everyone should apply filters to their inboxes.

First, you purposefully procrastinate looking at messages that are of lesser importance. Even if you stay subscribed to store deals, social updates and newsletters, you shouldn't go through all of these at the same time. By filtering them into a separate folder, you look at them at your leisure without occupying precious time that should be dedicated to important messages.

Second, you create a level of priority before you even look at a message. When you flag certain emails (like the ones from your boss), they'll show up at the top of your inbox. This allows you to focus on the most important messages fist before doing anything else.

Previously, we talked about the importance of moving some types of collaboration to another platform. When you get in the habit of having short, actionable conversations, you'll save a lot of wasted time in your inbox. Now it's time to talk about the ninth and final step of the process.

Step #9: Move Collaboration Elsewhere

While email is great for getting quick answers, it's not the best tool for collaborative projects. If you work on detailed projects or often need to communicate with multiple people simultaneously, then it's better to use collaborative tools.

Why should you move collaboration away from email? The biggest reason is to avoid the lengthy email conversations that often clutter an inbox. When you're dealing with multiple people, it's hard to know who is working on what or how a project is coming along.

The benefit of using collaborative tools is every member of your group can meet in a virtual location and discuss what needs to be done on a particular project.

Depending on the nature of your job or business, there is an assortment of tools that can be used for effective communication. Some integrate with email, while others come with their own dedicated platform. Here are six tools you can use for collaboration.

Tool 1: Calendar tools (Google/Outlook)

Using multiple calendars is like having multiple inboxes—they're hard to maintain on a consistent basis. In order to coordinate the people on your team, it's best to pick one universal calendar and stick with it.

The two most popular tools are Google Calendar (https://www.google.com/calendar) and Outlook Calendar (http://bit.ly/M08SCv). With these nifty calendars, you set your personal appointments, business meetings, and holidays and have other team members do the same. You can also create specific colors for certain team members or even use a special color for an important event. Do whatever works for your team (or family members).

By coordinating calendars, you can easily tell when team members are busy or away. You can use this type of tool to set meetings, schedule phone conversations, create deadlines and receive updates about a certain task.

While a calendar might seem like a simplistic solution to collaborating, having a central location for everyone's schedule will prevent you and your team members from exchanging pointless emails about their availability for a certain date and time.

Tool 2: Outsourcing Collaboration

If you run a virtual business (like me), then outsourcing can save you a lot of time. Unfortunately, coordinating with freelancers can also become a huge time suck if you have to send a lot of back-and-forth messages. The simpler solution is to use the mail interface that's offered by the most popular outsourcing sites.

For instance, Elance (http://www.elance.com), oDesk (http://www.odesk.com) and Freelancer (http://www.freelancer.com) all come with collaboration tools where you can get updates on specific projects. My suggestion is to turn off the email notifications from these sites and develop the habit of checking in a few times per day. Simply go through each current project, see what's been done and provide instructions for the next action item. I've done this for the last six months and it's saved me a bunch of time.

Tool 3: Basecamp or Hyperoffice

Lots of companies offer fee-based solutions for collaborative projects. The most popular of the bunch is Basecamp. With a total of over eight million projects managed, this is the tool that most businesses rely upon.

There are a lot of benefits to using Basecamp. Primarily, it offers a central location for tasks, to-do lists, files and all ongoing communication. Instead of having to worry about losing an important file or conversation thread, all team members can meet up on Basecamp and work together toward perfect project completion.

Hyperoffice (http://www.hyperoffice.com/) is similar to Basecamp in many ways. The biggest difference is it has a few added layers, including more interaction over their social platform. While I haven't personally used Hyperoffice, I've heard good things about this program.

Tool 4: Online Surveys

Sometimes you just want to poll multiple people without having to go through the hassle of receiving and reading lots of email messages. An easy way to do this is to create a simple online survey that everyone answers. That way, everyone can vote and you'll get the results back in an easy-to-understand graph. My preference for creating simple polls is the Survey Monkey (http://surveymonkey.com/) website, which has a free option.

Tool 5: Wikis

Wikis can be a great place to maintain a large pool of resources. They are a great place to put training and important documents. All a member has to do is access the wiki to get the latest information on a specific process. Wikis work like many online collaboration tools, except most of these programs are free. To get started, I recommend the Wikia website. (http://www.wikia.com/Special:CreateNewWiki)

Tool 6: Phone or Skype

Never forget the power of having a simple phone conversation. Nowadays, it doesn't matter if someone is halfway around the world. With Skype (http://www.skype.com), you can call another person's Skype account and not pay a dime.

We've come to the end of the step-by-step portion of this book, but we still have a few more tips and tools you can use to cut down on your inbox time. Let's get to them.

5 Quick Tips for Saving Time on Email

Want to completely minimize your email time? If so, there are a few "extra" tips you can use to speed up the process. While the following five tips are completely optional, you might find that they can help you get to an empty inbox on a daily basis.

Tip 1: Use signatures.

I'm sure you know all about email signatures—it's not like they're a big secret. Some people use them as a place for an inspiring quote or a funny joke, but this is a waste of space. Instead, use the signature file to convey helpful information to the recipient.

What I recommend is to include information that will answer any follow-up questions a recipient might have: important URLs, a link to a Frequently Asked Questions (FAQ) page and even your phone number (if you prefer to have quick conversations).
Include as much information as possible, and you'll avoid wasting time because people will be able to answer their own questions.

Tip 2: Add files to Dropbox.

In Step #5, I recommended using a central location for the common files that people ask for via email. My "bonus" tip here is to use <u>Dropbox</u> for this action. Simply click (or hover) on a specific item in this folder and you'll see the "Share Link" option. When you select it, Dropbox will automatically *copy* it to your clipboard. Then all you have to do is *paste* the link into an email.

The great thing about Dropbox is you can send files from any platform—any time and from wherever you are in the world. Once it's there, the file will always be virtually available whenever it is needed.

Tip 3: Use tabs, not windows.

Using tabs is pretty basic, but it can save you a lot of time if you're not already doing it. Opening a separate window for each Web page is horribly inefficient because you have to find the Web browser icon, click it and then go to the page. With a tab, you use a simple shortcut to open it up: Command-click (for the mac), middle-click (on a PC mouse), or CTRL+T if you're on a laptop.

Tip 4: Set up a distribution list.

If you're always sending emails to multiple people, it makes sense to create a distribution list for certain groups. That way, you can send a message with a single click instead of trying to hunt down everyone's contact information.

Tip 5: Learn keyboard shortcuts.

Keyboard shortcuts can save you *a lot* of typing time. Instead of having to scroll to the top of a screen, you can use simple commands for the commonly used actions on your computer.

Here are a few simple ones for Windows: CTRL+C is Copy, CTRL+X is Cut, CTRL+V is Paste, CTRL+Z is Undo, CTRL+B is Bold, CTRL+U is Underline and CTRL+I is Italicize.

There's a lot more you can do with Apple, so I recommend you check out (and print) this page (http://support.apple.com/kb/ht1343).

7 Tools for Achieving an Empty Inbox

While the purpose of this book is to teach you the *habit* of emptying your inbox every day, you can use software to achieve this goal. In this section, we'll talk about seven different tools that help along the way. You don't necessarily have to use all of them. Instead, I encourage you to check out each one and see if it can shave minutes off of your email processing time.

Tool 1: Evernote

I've already mentioned Evernote (http://www.evernote.com), but it's worth bringing up again. I use Evernote as my personal "ubiquitous idea capture device." Not only is it good for recording messages and ideas, it also fully syncs between mobile and desktop devices. This means I can record an idea in my car and have it accessible when I'm in front of my computer.

How is Evernote helpful for streamlining your inbox efforts? It can handle email services, collaboration ideas, reminders and anything that might be important for your job. If you're running errands and suddenly remember that you have to email someone, then you can create an "Email Reminders" folder on Evernote and have the list ready to go when processing your inbox.

Tool 2: Sanebox

Sanebox (http://www.Sanebox.com) is a third-party program that works with all email clients. Its purpose is to only allow important messages to show up in your inbox. The rest are sent to a separate folder. Then at the end of the day (or a time that you specify), it will send you a message that contains everything in the "separate" folder.

The main point behind this tool is to rate the emails you receive based on your personal reads, replies and when you mark things "up" as important. Therefore, the more you use the system, the more accurate it becomes.

Tool 3: Mailstrom

Mailstrom (https://mailstrom.co/) is a tool that brings sanity to an out-of-control inbox. It's designed to work alongside your existing email, with some functionality similar to that of Sanebox. Basically it uses your contact lists, delivered emails and messages read to raise or lower the visibility of the emails that you receive. That way, you can deal with the "low priority" emails *after* you've tackled the important ones.

What UnrollMe (http://www.unroll.me/) offers is a simple tool that hunts down all your subscriptions so you can look at them in a single email, unsubscribe from unwanted lists or ignore the email and keep it "as is." If you find yourself bombarded with too many sales-oriented emails, then UnrollMe can help you cut through the inbox clutter.

I Have 10,000 Emails! What Do I Do?

When I first developed the "decluttered inbox habit," I wrote about the experience on my blog. One reader—Susan J. Campbell (Amazon Author and Founder of the Weight Loss Laboratory [http://www.WeightLossLaboratory.com])—wrote the following in the comments section:

"Hey SJ, I have probably 10,000 email messages in my inbox. In your book, maybe you could include a section about getting from 10k down to zero before you even attempt the day-to-day strategy?"

I'll admit having 10,000 emails in your inbox can be pretty daunting. In fact, *none* of the strategies we've talked about so far will work if you have to deal with thousands of emails. Really, the only way to get to zero emails is to look at your email like a cluttered house—you can clean out the messages by taking consistent action on a daily basis. Here is a 10-step strategy to make that happen.

Step 1: Dedicate 30 Minutes per Day

There's no way you can process thousands of emails in a single day. Even if you could, it'll become such a mind-numbing activity that you'll probably give up after a few hours.

The secret? Think like someone cleaning a house—focus on taking consistent action (30 minutes) every single day. It doesn't matter *when* you do it—morning or night—simply schedule a block of time every day to work on clearing your inbox.

Step 2: Create the "Declutter Habit"

It's not enough to set aside 30 minutes per day; you have to commit to this process by turning it into a habit. You can do this by using the <u>Lift.do app</u>, signing up for a habit (like "Reduce inbox email count") and checking in every day. You'll find it easier to stick to this new routine if you're being held accountable for following through.

Step 3: Sign up for Unroll.me

Think of your inbox like *triage*. You need to take decisive action and stop the bleeding before doing anything else. The first way to do this is to sign up for the service <u>Unroll.me</u> and group all advertising emails into a single message. Use this daily digest to quickly unsubscribe from and eliminate the emails that offer no value.

Step 4: Sort by Sender

Every email provider gives you the ability to sort email by the sender (the big exception is Gmail, but this article provides a decent workaround: http://bit.ly/1gEAlne). When you first get started, select this option to group all your messages into similar categories. This will make it easy to quickly do the next step.

Step 5: "Mass Delete" Junk Messages

The biggest culprits in your inbox are likely groups of advertising messages, social media updates and emails from various accounts (like your bank). You want to "select all" on each group of messages and get rid of them.

Use your judgment for what gets deleted here. If you think something might be important, then put it into a "documents" folder instead of trashing it.

Repeat this step for all advertising messages in your inbox. If something was sent five months ago, you're probably not going to take action on it, so the best thing to do is to get rid of it.

Step 6: Reply on Other Platforms

We often save messages from Facebook and other social media sites to act as a reminder to respond to somebody. Now is the time to eliminate this habit. Instead of using your inbox as a to-do list, develop a routine where you "check in" a few times per day and respond to any updates and personal emails.

Step 7: File Important Emails

Create a series of folders that best fit your job and personal life. Use these to store messages that might be important in the future. It really doesn't matter what you label them—what's important is to stop using your inbox like an archive. If an email contains crucial information, then file it away.

Step 8: Reply to Individual People

At this point, you will have cleared a lot of the clutter in your inbox. It might have taken you a few hours or a few weeks. The good news is you'll be left with a fraction of what you had when you first started. In this step, you'll reply to messages that require a personal response.

The trick to this step is to sort by sender (like in step #3). Find all the messages from a single person, copy and paste what they discussed into a Notepad file and then write a detailed response.

I do realize that this step can be painful to some. You might have "ignored" certain people and let their emails go unanswered. Honestly, I found a simple *sorry* works with most people. Trust me; we all get swamped by having too much to do. The recipient should understand that life happens and it's easy to get overwhelmed.

Step 9: Keep at It

The previous step might take a long time to complete. You might get frustrated because the end never seems in sight. My advice is to stick to the habit and take action on a consistent basis. Slowly, but surely, you'll find the pile of emails will slowly be reduced and eliminated.

Step 10: Avoid Making the Same Mistake

Once you finally reach that "zero milestone" in your inbox, take time to enjoy the moment and then never again let yourself get buried under a pile of email. Simply practice the strategies I outlined in this book and set aside time each day to fully process and single-handle each message that comes your way.

Final Thoughts

Well, that's it for this book. You now have a blueprint for decluttering your inbox and keeping it that way. If you *apply* these lessons, you'll reduce the stress of having to process dozens of messages that all seem important. You'll make quick decisions, provide concise responses and process your inbox in a shorter amount of time.

In every book, I urge the reader to take action. Now I mean it more than ever. If you've gotten to this point, then that means the clutter in your inbox has become a real problem. That's why you need to take aggressive action and clear out your inbox.

To get started, let me recap what you've learned with a simple action plan:

1. Read and understand the six limiting beliefs about email.
2. Develop one of the seven habits for managing email each month.
3. Turn off email notifications on your phone.
4. Disable other notifications and distractions.

5. Streamline all your inboxes into one, maybe two, locations.
6. Practice the 4 D's when processing emails.
7. Create a central location for commonly used files.
8. Write template responses and use software to handle common questions.
9. Practice the "10 Rules" to write efficient emails.
10. Organize your inbox by creating email filters.
11. Move collaboration out of your inbox.
12. Save even more time by implementing the five quick email tips.
13. Download and try the seven tools for achieving an empty inbox.

Decluttering your inbox on a daily basis is like any other habit. At first, it'll be challenging and hard to do every day. But when you do it on a consistent basis, instinct will kick in. Eventually you'll do it in an efficient manner and end every day with zero messages sitting in your inbox.

Steve Scott
http://www.DevelopGoodHabits.com

Would You Like to Know More?

Often it's easy to procrastinate on a major task like decluttering your inbox. You ignore this problem because you're paralyzed by uncertainty and what's required to make it happen.

One way to fix this problem is to adopt an "anti-procrastination" mindset. When you know *how* to take action on a consistent basis, you can systematically accomplish any goal. In my book, *23 Anti-Procrastination Habits*, you'll get a series of simple-to-follow routines that can help not only clear your inbox, but can increase your productivity in many different areas.

You can learn more here
http://www.developgoodhabits.com/book-23aph

Thank You

Before you go, I'd like to say "thank you" for purchasing my guide.

I know you could have picked from dozens of books on habit development, but you took a chance with my system.

So a big thanks for ordering this book and reading all the way to the end.

Now I'd like ask for a *small* favor. Could you please take a minute or two and leave a review for this book on Amazon?

http://www.developgoodhabits.com/declutter-inbox

This feedback will help me continue to write the kind of books that help you get results. And if you loved it, then please let me know :-)

More Books by S.J. Scott

- *23 Anti-Procrastination Habits: How to Stop Being Lazy and Get Results In Your Life*

- *Writing Habit Mastery: How to Write 2,000 Words a Day and Forever Cure Writer's Block*

- *Wake Up Successful: How to Increase Your Energy and Achieve Any Goal with a Morning Routine*

- *10,000 Steps Blueprint: The Daily Walking Habit for Healthy Weight Loss and Lifelong Fitness*

- *70 Healthy Habits: How to Eat Better, Feel Great, Get More Energy and Live a Healthy Lifestyle*

- *Resolutions That Stick! How 12 Habits Can Transform Your New Year*

About the Author

"Build a Better Life - One Habit at a Time"

Getting more from life doesn't mean following the latest diet craze or motivation program. True success happens when you take action on a daily basis. In other words, it's your habits that help you achieve goals and live the life you've always wanted.

In his books, S.J. provides daily action plans for every area of your life: health, fitness, work and personal relationships. Unlike other personal development guides, his content focuses on taking action. So instead of reading over-hyped strategies that rarely work in the real-world, you'll get information that can be immediately implemented

When not writing, S.J. likes to read, exercise and explore the different parts of the world.

Made in the USA
San Bernardino, CA
26 June 2014